Begin in English

Vocabulary-Expanding Short Stories
for
Launched Beginners

VOLUME 1

Stories by Judith Bailey

Illustrations by Julian Smedley

Edited by Joan Ashkenas

JAG PUBLICATIONS

Published by:
 JAG Publications
11288 Ventura Blvd.
Studio City, CA 91604
Telephone and Fax: (818) 505-9002
info@jagpublications-esl.com

Design by Words & Deeds, San Jose
Production by Jack Lanning

Printed in the United States of America

Library of Congress catalog card no. 87-81968

ISBN 0-943327-04-0

10   9   8   7   6

Revised 4th Edition 1998

Remembering Edward

FOREWORD:
To the instructor

These fourteen stories are designed for easy, entertaining reading by launched beginners of English: for those who now have some English vocabulary and are familiar with the present tense. The stories have all been tested in the classroom. One of the great delights for my students, and for me, was their discovery that they already knew enough English to read an entire story.

Subject matter is quite varied. There are folk tales retold, human interest stories, some humor, some biography, history and even a mystery. A major attribute of all of them is that they really give the student something of substance to read—a short story or play, rather than simply a paragraph or two.

It hardly needs to be argued that these days our classrooms are filled with students from a multitude of language backgrounds. But teachers, generally, are not multi-lingual. It follows then, that we teachers can help our students help themselves by becoming adept at using the dictionary. Students are provided here with a useful beginner's vocabulary, and emphasis is placed on teaching and encouraging use of the bilingual dictionary.

Not necessarily second in order of importance is that familiarity with the dictionary is basic to literacy. Although most foreign language students use bilingual dictionaries at beginning levels of their studies, some do not know how. I feel very strongly that these students should own them, and be taught to use them right away. I say this first as a foreign language student, and only second as a language teacher. Admittedly, it can be intrusive to stop and slavishly consult the dictionary for each word. But frequently, context conveys meaning, making it unnecessary to look up every unfamiliar word. This is ideal, but not always the case, and students indeed need to look up new words from time to time. There is really nothing like it for rapidly increasing vocabulary and getting on with the story.

REGARDING DICTIONARY WORK

Because I feel it is so important that students be comfortable with the dictionary, I have included at the beginning of the book a step-by-step dictionary lesson. It assumes that the student needs help with the basic concept of alphabetizing. I found that this part is very easily understood, and paves the way for the next part, "Using the Dictionary." During the lesson I work closely with the students and read along with them, pointing out the words and letters of the words they are looking up, so they may grasp the idea of alphabetical order. It may take up to an hour or so to teach, depending on the students' backgrounds, and on class size. But the rewards of this exercise will be immediately evident.

REGARDING VOCABULARY AND WORD LISTS

The vocabulary contained here is highly controlled. It includes words from the *The 2,000 Most Frequently Used Words In English,* edited by Robert J. Dixson. In this resource, the first 500 words follow the Thorndike-Lorge list. The second 500 words were derived, with some modification, mainly from the *Interim Report On Vocabulary Selection For Teaching Of English As A Foreign Language* (Palmer, Thorndike, West, Sapir, etc.). The remaining 1000 words of this list were compiled from Thorndike, emphasizing assessed needs for teaching conversation in English to primary level students.

In order to facilitate the reading and augment the word list, there has also been included vocabulary from the *Oxford Picture Dictionary of American English.* Obviously, a picture dictionary, whatever its limits, is "universal": using pictures labeled in English to serve ESL students of every language background. Nearly all of the words used in the word list, and those which are most likely to be new to some students, are found in one or both of these resources.

The beautiful illustrations that accompany the stories are also designed to convey meaning.

In addition to this, for the benefit of Spanish speakers, there has been a special effort made to use cognates. Cognates are veritable vehicles for transferring similarities: psychological frames of reference, making for real ease of comprehension.

A comprehensive word list at the back of the book indicates which words are found in Dixson's high frequency list, which in Oxford's Picture Dictionary, and which are cognates of Spanish.

Stories are told in the present tense, and in the future using "going to", since these tenses are stressed during the first year of studies. The exercises here are not strictly "grammar work". That remains the burden of the core text being used in class. Instead, the focus is on vocabulary expansion, with dictionary work implied, reading comprehension and discussion.

My advanced beginning students have enjoyed these stories. More than that—they have clamored for them! I truly believe yours will, too.

Joan Ashkenas, Editor

PROCEDURE

READING

It is suggested that students be allowed to read the story through silently. Then, they may re-read it to pick out the unfamiliar vocabulary. Usually, upon this second reading, much will be understood through context and by reference to the illustrations. After that, students should be encouraged to look up words independently in the dictionary. For the first story or so, you may wish to offer extra help to those students with newly acquired dictionary skills. Then, you might ask the class to follow along as you read aloud. For extra practice, students can be asked to each read a passage orally, around the room. The large illustrations preceding each story work well at this point for group discussions. They mainly depict pivotal scenes. Students might be asked questions: "who?", "what?", "where?", "when?". Or they could be asked to describe scenes in their own words, saying, "This is a...

EXERCISES

I. Vocabulary List. The words selected here for study should be quite familiar after the readings and the dictionary work. They are listed to ensure that is the case. Also, some words are used again in successive stories in slightly different contexts.

II. Definitions. (See Answer Key at back of book). A real opportunity for vocabulary expansion is in this exercise. Here, the most challenging words from the above list have been selected. For students who wish to do so, a chance is provided to explore the dictionary and learn synonyms for words they have now studied.

You may wish students to check their own work, but you may find it preferable to discuss the answers with the class as a whole, since many of the words have multiple usage.

III. Reading Comprehension. (See Answer Key at back of book.) This exercise consists of questions to be answered by referring to the story and copying the correct passage. Its purpose is for practice in writing and spelling, as well as for comprehension. As in Exercise II above, you may want students to check their own work.

IV. Discussion. Students are asked to look at pictures and, using the vocabulary, answer questions. These are especially good for paired students, but can be used for group work as well. Students should have acquired some confidence after the initial readings and vocabulary drill, to talk with others about the situations and characters.

V. Writing. After the above oral work, students are asked to perform some original written exercises: (a) to list several things about the story or characters. In answering these, some students may be able and motivated to use original language. Others could answer the questions according to their ability, in just a word or short phrase from the story itself. You will have to be the judge of individual competency. But, since enjoyment of reading is of primary consideration here, you may not want to frighten off those less able students with an exacting writing requirement. Or (b) to write from dictation. For this, ask students to study a particular paragraph from the story, then close the book and write as you dictate. This might be a new activity for many. It is suggested that each sentence be repeated slowly, first all the way through, and then in short phrases. It may be necessary to read it a third time. Advise students to note spelling and punctuation, especially if dialogue is included.

AS A COMPLEMENT TO THE LAUBACH METHOD:

Begin in English, though designed for non-English-speaking students, can also be used effectively by English speakers for remedial work in basic reading, writing and spelling. It is particularly appropriate for students of the Laubach Method at Skill Book levels 2 and 3. This book's added dimension is that it teaches and encourages use of the foreign student's own bilingual dictionary, or the native speaker's English dictionary.

A great number of the chart-listed skills at levels 2 and 3 are again introduced or reinforced here. The exercises test reading comprehension, and offer practice in spelling. Writing practice is provided, sometimes by dictation, sometimes by copying sentences for reinforcement, sometimes by referring to the text, other times in original sentences, as individual abilities allow.

The underlying intent here is, as in the Laubach Method, motivation of independent learning with a minimum of teaching help.

CONTENTS

Learning to Use the Dictionary

I ALPHABETIZING

Use the alphabet to help you do the following exercises.

a b c d e f g h i j k l m n o p q r s t u v w x y z

1. Put these letters in correct order:

b c a   ____   ____   ____

i g h   ____   ____   ____

o m n   ____   ____   ____

2. Put these words in correct order according to their first letters:

| sit | baby | light | house | ____ ____ ____ ____ |
| fast | apple | cake | down | ____ ____ ____ ____ |

3. These words have the same first letter. Arrange them according to their second letters:

buy	big	boy		____ ____ ____
pin	pan	put	pet	____ ____ ____ ____
shell	sell	spell		____ ____ ____

4. These words begin with the same two letters. Put them in order according to their third letters:

plan	plum	plot	____ ____ ____
flock	flake	flute	____ ____ ____
street	stamp	stop	____ ____ ____
through	thought	thin	____ ____ ____

II USING THE DICTIONARY

Open the dictionary to where the letter 'b' begins. Notice that the first words you see following the 'b' all have 'a' for their second letter. Now look at their third letter. Notice that these third letters follow in alphabetical order: first 'a', then 'b', then 'c', through the rest of the alphabet. Using this idea, let's practice and look up the following words: baby, back, bad, bag.

Now turn the pages and pass the letters 'ba' until you find words beginning with 'be.' Look up these words: beach, bed, before, begin.

Now continue turning pages until you find words starting with 'bi.' Find these words: bicycle, big, bill, bird.

Now look for these words: black, boat, brake, bud.

III DICTIONARY WORK

Open the dictionary and look at the top of any page. You can see two words in dark letters. The word on the left gives you the first word on the page. The word on the right gives you the last word on the page, and between these, all words are in alphabetical order, according to their second, third, fourth, etc. letters.

Let's practice finding some words. Turn to the letter 'b' and look for the word 'bad.' You know it is close to the beginning of the 'b' because its second letter is 'a.' It comes after words beginning with 'bab' and 'bac' because 'b' and 'c' come before 'd' in the alphabet.

Let's try another word. Turn to the letter 'n' and find the word 'not.' The second letter, 'o', of 'not' is more towards the middle of the alphabet, so you must pass words beginning with 'na', 'ne', 'ni', and find words beginning with 'no.' Now you need to find the third letter, 't', after the 'o.' Look for it in its alphabetical order at the top of the pages in dark letters.

Using what you know, you can now look up any new words in the dictionary as you read.

At 4 o'clock when Tony comes home from work the house is full of police, TV cameras and reporters.

A Useless Old Man

Every morning, Bruno's daughter-in-law pushes his wheelchair to the window. The daughter-in-law's name is Eva. She is married to Bruno's son, Tony. Before she goes to work, Eva gives Bruno breakfast. She puts his binoculars near him. She makes him a sandwich for lunch.

Eva does these things because Tony goes to work too early to do them. Eva likes Bruno. She is sad that he does not like himself. Because he cannot walk and cannot work, Bruno thinks he is a useless old man.

Just before she goes to work, Eva puts the telephone near Bruno.

In Italian, she says, "Papa, if you have a problem, call me. It's okay to call me at the office. Let me show you again how to dial the number."

Eva knows Bruno does not want to use the telephone. He speaks very little English and he is ashamed.

After Eva goes, Bruno picks up his binoculars. He begins to look for his only friends, the birds. From his window, Bruno can see the park. Every day he looks for birds near the trees. He is interested in birds.

At twelve o'clock, Bruno eats his sandwich. He is lonely. He loves birds, but they talk only to each other. Sometimes, Bruno wants somebody to talk to him.

With his binoculars, Bruno looks at people in the park. Some very small children are playing in the sandbox. A little boy throws sand at a girl. She cries.

"Maybe she has sand in her eyes," Bruno thinks. Then he tells himself, "It's not your business, old man. Her mother is there."

Bruno moves the binoculars. Two fourteen year old boys are smoking cigarettes on a park bench.

"Those two bad boys belong in school," Bruno thinks. Then he tells himself, "It's not your business, old man."

He moves the binoculars again. A young man and a pretty girl are kissing under a tree. Bruno thinks, "Ah, love is beautiful, but it is not your business, old man."

Bruno moves the binoculars again. He sees a man running. A woman is running after him, but she can't run fast. The man is holding something. Bruno follows him with the binoculars. Now he can see that the man is running with a woman's purse.

"Oh, my God, he is a robber," Bruno says. "He is taking that woman's purse! Yes, yes, I know this is my business. But what can I do? I am a useless old man!"

The robber jumps into a car and begins to drive away. Bruno can read the license number with his binoculars. He has a pen, but no paper. He writes the license number on the palm of his hand. When he looks up, the robber and his car are gone.

"Now what can I do?" Bruno asks himself. He knows what to do, but it is difficult for him to do it.

"You must do it, old man," Bruno tells himself. He picks up the phone. Slowly and carefully he dials the number of Eva's office. He hopes Eva answers the phone.

"Hello?" Eva says.

Bruno tells her, "Eva, call the police...."

At 4 o'clock when Tony comes home from work the house is full of police, TV cameras and reporters. Eva is helping Bruno tell the reporters about the robber. Bruno still has the robber's license number on the palm of his hand. Because of Bruno's quick thinking, the robber is now in jail.

Bruno is on the 9 o'clock news. All the neighbors come to visit and admire the hero.

"Do you still think you're useless?" Tony asks.

Bruno smiles. "Maybe not."

He feels happy. One of the neighbors speaks Italian. He is coming tomorrow to play cards.

Exercises

I   Vocabulary
You probably know many of these words from reading the story and looking at the pictures. If there are still some you don't know, look them up in your dictionary now.

useless	wheelchair	ashamed	problem	follow
lonely	license	belong	palm	
(play) cards	hero	jail	neighbor	

II   Definitions
Try to guess the best definition for these words. Then look them up in your dictionary and draw a circle around the answer.

1. useless
   - a. not good for anything
   - b. not happy about anything
   - c. not hoping for anything

2. ashamed
   - a. alone
   - b. embarrassed
   - c. angry

3. belong (in)
   - a. to answer a question
   - b. to travel somewhere
   - c. to be part of something

4. reporter
   - a. a kind of teacher
   - b. a kind of doctor
   - c. a kind of writer

5. lonely
   - a. ashamed
   - b. happy
   - c. alone

6. hero
   - a. a kind man
   - b. a brave man
   - c. a wise man

III   Reading Comprehension
Read the questions. Find the answers in the story. Write the answers under the questions.
1. What does Eva do before she goes to work?

_____

_____

2. Why does Bruno think he is a useless old man?

_____

_____

3. Why doesn't Bruno want to use the telephone?

_____

_____

4. Through his binoculars, Bruno sees a young man and a pretty girl. What are they doing?

_____

_____

5. Where does Bruno write the license number of the robber's car?

_____

_____

6. What does Bruno say to Eva when he talks to her on the telephone?

_____

_____

IV   Discussion
Look at the pictures. Talk to your partner.
Use words from the story.

Picture #1.
What is Eva showing
Bruno?
Why is it difficult for
Bruno to call Eva?

18

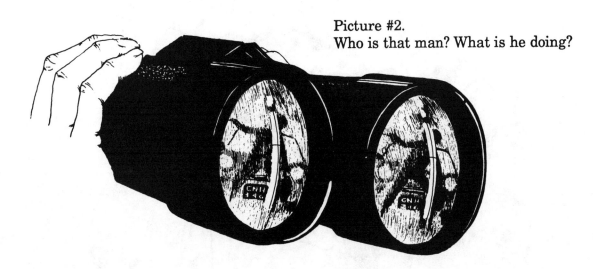

Picture #2.
Who is that man? What is he doing?

V   Writing
Write three or more things that Bruno sees with his binoculars.

1. _____

2. _____

3. _____

4. _____

5. _____

The farmer carries one end of the pole and the boy carries the other end.

The Man, the Boy and the Donkey
(An Old Folk Tale)

A farmer and his son are going to town. They walk down the road with their donkey. The sun is hot, and the sky is blue. It is a good day for walking.

After one or two miles, they meet a man. The man looks at them and shakes his head. He says, "You fools, don't you know what a donkey is for? A donkey is to ride on."

The farmer does not want anyone to think he is a fool. He puts his son on the donkey's back. Then the farmer, the boy and the donkey continue down the road to town again.

After two or three miles, they meet some men. The men look at the farmer, the boy and the donkey. Then they look at each other and shake their heads. One of them says to the son, "What a lazy boy you are! Aren't you ashamed to let your poor father walk while you ride?"

The farmer does not want his son to feel ashamed. He tells the boy to get off. This time the farmer gets on the donkey's back. Then the farmer, his son and the donkey continue down the road to town again.

After three or four miles, they meet two women. The women look at the farmer, the boy and the donkey. Then they look at each and shake their heads. One woman asks the other, "What do you think of a father who rides on a donkey and lets his poor little son walk?"

"I think he is a bad father," the second woman says.

The farmer doesn't want anyone to think he is a bad father, but he doesn't know what to do. He thinks and he thinks. Then he puts the boy in back of him on the donkey. Now they are both riding to town.

As they ride down the road, people come out of their houses to look at them. The people look and talk to each other, and shake their heads.

The farmer asks, "Why are you all shaking your heads?"

One of the people says, "Aren't you ashamed? A great big man and a fat, lazy boy, both riding on that poor little donkey?"

The farmer and his son quickly get off the donkey. They don't want to be ashamed, but they don't know what to do. They sit down on the road and think and think for a long time. Finally, they decide to tie the donkey's feet to a big wooden pole and carry him. The farmer carries one end of the pole and the boy carries the other end. The unhappy donkey hangs upside-down between them kicking his feet. In this way, they walk into town.

When the people of the town see the two fools carrying a donkey, they all laugh. Soon the whole town is laughing.

The farmer and his son carry the donkey across a bridge. The donkey continues kicking and kicking, and now he gets his feet untied. He jumps off the bridge into the river and swims away, never to return. The farmer and the boy are very unhappy. Their good donkey is lost and they have to walk home without him.

The people of the town shake their heads as they see the foolish farmer and his son walking home without their donkey at the end of a long, hot day. For many years after, they tell the story of the man, the boy and the donkey.

THE LESSON: People who try to please everyone don't please anyone.

Exercises

I   Vocabulary
You probably know many of these words from reading the story and looking at the pictures. If there are still some you don't know, look them up in your dictionary now.

shake	fools	lazy	ashamed	decide
tie	pole	unhappy	kick	tie
laugh	cross	bridge	jump	
swim	lost	(to) please		

II   Definitions
Try to guess the best definition for these words. Then look them up in your dictionary and draw a circle around the answer.

1. shake
    a. to touch
    b. to break
    c. to move

2. fool
    a. a person who is sad
    b. a person who is polite
    c. a person who is stupid

3. lazy (boy)
    a. a boy who likes to work
    b. a boy who doesn't eat much
    c. a boy who doesn't like to work

4. (to) cross
    a. to go inside
    b. to go over
    c. to go away

5. lost
    a. at home
    b. lonely
    c. missing

6. (to) please
    a. to make people laugh
    b. to make people nervous
    c. to make people happy

III   Reading Comprehension
Read the questions. Find the answers in the story. Write the answers under the questions.

1. Where are the farmer and his son going?

_____

_____

2. The first man they meet tells them what a donkey is for. What does he say?

_____

_____

3. What does the farmer do after he tells the boy to get off the donkey?

_____

_____

4. What does the second woman say about the farmer?

_____

_____

5. What do the farmer and his son do after they both get off the donkey?

_____

_____

6. What does the donkey do when he gets his feet untied?

_____

_____

IV Discussion
Look at the pictures. Talk to your partner. Use words from the story.

Picture #1.
Why is the farmer
ashamed?
What are they
thinking?
What do they
decide to do?

Picture #2.
How does the donkey get his feet untied?
Can people please everyone always?

V Writing

Write three things the people say to the farmer and the boy as they continue down the road to town.

1. _____

2. _____

3. _____

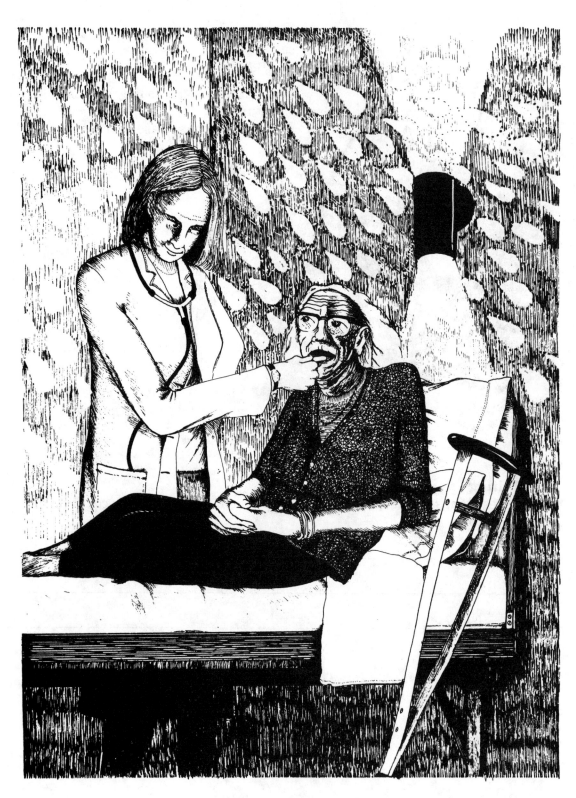

"Say 'Ah,' please."

Mrs. Proctor Goes to the Doctor
A Comedy

CHARACTERS

Dr. Dunne, *a young doctor wearing her white coat*

Mrs. Proctor, *93 years old, a tiny little woman who has to walk with a crutch*

THE SCENE

Dr. Dunne's office. Mrs. Proctor is sitting on the examination table.

DR. DUNNE:	*(She puts a stick in Mrs. Proctor's mouth.)* Say 'Ah,' please.
MRS. PROCTOR:	Aaahhh!
DR. DUNNE:	*(She listens to Mrs. Proctor's heart with a stethoscope.)* Breathe in, please. Thank you. *(She looks into Mrs. Proctor's left eye. Then she looks into her right eye.)* Mrs. Proctor, may I ask you how old you are?
MRS. PROCTOR:	I am ninety-three years old, Doctor.
DR. DUNNE:	Ninety-three? Isn't that wonderful! Tell me, Mrs. Proctor, do you have any pain?
MRS. PROCTOR:	Doctor, I have terrible pain, all the time.
DR. DUNNE:	Where is the pain?
MRS. PROCTOR:	Where is it? My head hurts as if somebody is hitting it with hammer.
DR. DUNNE:	*(She writes down what Mrs. Proctor says.)* Pain in head. Where else do you have pain?

27

MRS. PROCTOR: Where? Everywhere. My feet hurt. My back hurts. My stomach hurts. My neck hurts. My hands hurt. That's not all. Some of my teeth hurt.

DR. DUNNE: *(She is writing what Mrs Proctor tells her as fast as she can.)* Feet. Back. Stomach. Neck. *(Now she stops writing and looks at Mrs. Proctor with a smile.)* Mrs. Proctor, when people live to be ninety-three years old, they get some little pains here and there. That's the way life is. There isn't much anyone can do for you.

MRS. PROCTOR: Are you saying that you can't help me?

DR. DUNNE: Mrs. Proctor, I am only a doctor. I am not God. I can't make you grow younger.

MRS. PROCTOR: I am not asking you to make me grow younger. What I want is to grow OLDER!

Exercises

I   Vocabulary

You probably know many of these words from reading the story and looking at the pictures. If there are still some you don't know, look them up in your dictionary now.

comedy	character(s)	scene	examination
crutch	stethoscope	young	old
stick	hammer	breathe	pain
hurt	grow (old/young)		

II   Definitions

Try to guess the best definition for these words. Then look them up in your dictionary and draw a circle around the answer.

1. comedy
   a. a sad story
   b. a difficult examination
   c. a funny story

2. scene
   a. a person in a comedy
   b. a place where something happens
   c. something to buy

3. crutch
   a. something to use for running
   b. something to use for sitting
   c. something to use for walking

4. breathe
   a. include
   b. increase
   c. inhale

5. (to have) pain
   a. to be tired
   b. to be sick
   c. to have a cold

6. (to grow) old
   a. to become cold
   b. to live long
   c. to be tall

III   Reading Comprehension

Read the questions. Find the answers in the story. Write the answers under the questions.

1. What does Mrs. Proctor use to walk?

2. Where is Mrs. Proctor sitting?

_____

_____

3. How does Dr. Dunne listen to Mrs. Proctor's heart?

_____

_____

4. When Dr. Dunne asks Mrs. Proctor how old she is, what does she say?

_____

_____

5. What is Dr. Dunne writing?

_____

_____

IV Discussion
Look at the pictures. Talk to your partner. Use words from the story.

Picture #1.
What is Dr.
Dunne
doing?
What is she
using?
What is
Mrs. Proctor
doing?

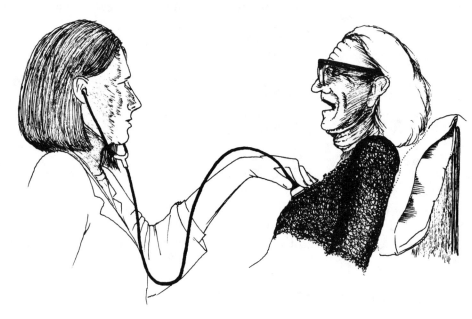

Picture #2.
What is Mrs. Proctor telling
Dr. Dunne?
What is Dr. Dunne answering?

V   Writing
Write three things that Dr. Dunne does to examine Mrs. Proctor.

1. _____

2. _____

3. _____

Can Dr. Dunne help Mrs. Proctor? Write two reasons why.

1. _____

2. _____

Sam offers the plate to Gary.

32

Cookies

Gary takes the elevator to the fifteenth floor of the office building. He is wearing a plain blue suit, a white shirt with a gray tie, and black shoes. Gary is twenty-two years old. He is nervous. He is going to talk to an important man about a job.

Gary gets off the elevator. A secretary asks him, "May I help you?"

He tells her that he is here to talk to Mr. Wilson about a job.

The secretary's name is Mrs. Fox. She says, "Mr. Wilson isn't back from lunch yet. Please sit down."

Gary sits on the sofa.

Sam takes the elevator to the fifteenth floor of the office building. He is wearing a bright colored sport jacket, a blue shirt, and an orange tie with purple flowers. Sam is twenty years old. He is excited. He is going to talk to an important man about a job.

Sam gets off the elevator. Mrs. Fox asks him, "May I help you?"

He tells her that he is here to talk to Mr. Wilson about a job.

Mrs. Fox thinks, "Both these young men want the same job."

She tells Sam, "Mr. Wilson isn't back from lunch yet. Please sit down."

Sam sits in a chair.

The two young men wait. While they wait, Gary looks quickly at Sam. Gary understands that he and Sam are trying to get the same job. He looks at Sam's bright clothes.

He thinks, "Some people certainly have very strange ideas about clothes."

Sam looks quickly at Gary. Sam, too, understands that he and Gary want the same job. He looks at Gary's plain blue suit, white shirt and gray tie. He thinks, "Some people certainly never have new ideas about clothes."

Mrs. Fox looks at the clock. She is unhappy because Mr. Wilson is late. She likes people to be on time.

"Do you want some coffee?" she asks Sam and Gary.

They both say yes. Mrs. Fox notices that there are still two cookies in her cookie box. She puts them on a plate and brings them with the coffee. One cookie is much smaller than the other.

Sam offers the plate to Gary.

"Oh, no. Please take one first," Gary says.

"OK." Sam takes the bigger cookie and puts it in his mouth.

"Don't you know," Gary asks, "that it is not polite to take the bigger cookie?"

Sam eats his cookie slowly, enjoying every bite. Then he says, "Let's imagine that both cookies are still on this plate. This time YOU are the first one to take a cookie. Which one do you take?"

"The smaller one, because I am polite," says Gary.

"But you HAVE the smaller cookie," Sam tells Gary, "so what are you complaining about?"

Mrs. Fox's telephone rings. Mr. Wilson is calling her to say that he is now in his office. Because it is so late, he wants to talk to Gary and Sam together.

Mrs. Fox smiles at them as they walk into Mr. Wilson's office.

"I wonder which one is going to get the job?" she thinks.

(To the reader: Which one do you think is going to get the job?)

Exercises

I   Vocabulary
You probably know many of these words from reading the story and looking at the pictures. If there are still some you don't know, look them up in your dictionary now.

elevator	plain	nervous	excited
bright	idea	unhappy	polite
imagine	complaining	wonder	

II   Definitions
Try to guess the best definition for these words. Then look them up in your dictionary and draw a circle around the answer.

1. excited
   a. angry
   b. emotional
   c. calm

2. nervous
   a. calm
   b. confident
   c. anxious

3. polite
   a. courteous
   b. hungry
   c. thirsty

4. idea
   a. a question
   b. a thought
   c. a pain

5. (to) imagine
   a. to want something
   b. to find something
   c. to have an idea about something

6. complain (about)
   a. talk about
   b. protest about
   c. laugh about

7. wonder
   a. know
   b. want to know
   c. find

III Reading Comprehension

Read the questions. Find the answers in the story. Write the answers under the questions.

1. Why is Gary nervous?

    _____

    _____

2. How old is Sam?

    _____

    _____

3. What does Sam tell Mrs. Fox?

    _____.

    _____

4. Why do Gary and Sam have to wait?

    _____

    _____

5. Where does Sam sit?

    _____

    _____

6. Why is Mrs. Fox unhappy?

    _____

    _____

IV Discussion

Look at the pictures. Talk to your partner. Use words from the story.

Picture #1.
How does Sam feel?
What is he thinking?
How does Gary feel?
What is he thinking?

Picture #2.
What is Mrs. Fox thinking?
Who do you think is going to get the job?

V Writing

Write three things you know about Gary from the story.

1. _____

2. _____

3. _____

Write three things you know about Sam from the story.

1. _____

2. _____

3. _____

"Not now, Jimmy."

A Present for Peter

The name of the store is "The Rock Shop." It's a small store, but many people come there to buy rocks and precious stones. Some people buy them for their scientific interest. Other people buy them just because they are beautiful.

Anna comes to the "The Rock Shop" to buy a present for her husband, Peter. Peter is interested in science and Anna wants to give him a beautiful rock for his birthday. After she looks at many, Anna buys a small piece of obsidian. She likes it because it is very black and very shiny. The man who works in the store tells her that obsidian is glass that comes from a volcano. He puts the obsidian in a paper bag and Anna goes out to wait for the bus.

On the bus, Anna sits next to a young mother and her baby. Anna smiles at the baby and talks to Susan, the mother. Anna wants to have a baby some day. She is so interested in the baby that she almost forgets to get off at her bus stop. At the last moment she rings the bell and jumps out. The doors close and the bus drives away.

Then Susan sees that Anna's paper bag is still on the seat. There is something hard in it. Susan calls to the bus driver, "Quick, stop the bus! This bag belongs to that pretty young woman. Look, you can still see her! She is crossing the street. Can't you stop the bus?"

"No, I can't," says the bus driver. "Do you want me to lose my job? Give the bag to me. I promise to take it to the office. If that young woman wants her bag, she can come there."

The bus driver is almost finished working. Soon she drives the empty bus to the bus station. She doesn't forget her promise, but she is curious to know what is in the bag, so she looks.

"Nothing but a rock," she thinks. "Who needs a rock? Nobody. If I take it to the office, they are going to think I'm foolish."

The bus driver throws the rock over a fence into a small park.

An hour later, a little boy named Jimmy is walking home from school. He sees the very black, very shiny rock under a tree. He picks it up and takes it home. He wants to show it to his mother.

Jimmy's mother doesn't have time to look. She says, "Not now, Jimmy. The painter is still here. He is just finishing the kitchen and I have to pay him. Anyway, I don't want you to bring any more dirty rocks into this house. Throw it away this instant!"

But Jimmy likes the shiny rock. He doesn't want to throw it away. There is an old jacket hanging in the closet. Jimmy thinks it is his father's jacket, and hides the rock in one of the pockets.

The jacket does not belong to Jimmy's father. It belongs to the painter. The painter gets ready to go home. He puts his ladder and paints into his truck. Then he remembers his jacket. He goes back to get it and throws it into the truck, too.

In his apartment, the painter sees that his wife has tears in her eyes.

"Happy birthday, Peter," says Anna very sadly. She tells him about the obsidian, the bus, and the woman with the baby. "I feel bad because I have no present for you," she says.

"Don't feel bad," Peter tells her. "Give me a kiss. That's the best birthday present. Let's go eat in a restaurant. Put on your coat while I get my jacket."

Peter comes back with his jacket. He has a very curious expression on his face.

"Anna," he says, "there is something in the pocket of my jacket that I want you to see..."

Exercises

I Vocabulary

You probably know many of these words from reading the story and looking at the pictures. If there are still some you don't know, look them up in your dictionary now.

rock   precious   stone   empty
promise   curious   foolish   fence
dirty   hang   hide   pocket
ladder   tear(s)   volcano

II Definitions

Try to guess the best definition for these words. Then look them up in your dictionary and draw a circle around the answer.

1. rock
    a. a small animal
    b. a piece of wood
    c. a stone

2. precious
    a. pretty
    b. valuable
    c. hard

3. empty
    a. not fat
    b. not hot
    c. not full

4. curious*
    a. strange
    b. beautiful
    c. inquisitive
    *two meanings: adjective and adverb

5. foolish
    a. sad
    b. happy
    c. silly

6. hang
    a. suspend
    b. dry
    c. stop

III Reading Comprehension

Read the questions. Find the answers in the story. Write the answers under the questions.

1. Why does Anna want to give Peter a rock for his birthday?

2. Why does Anna like obsidian?

_____

_____

3. What does the man who works in "The Rock Shop" tell Ann about obsidian?

_____

_____

4. Where does the bus driver throw the rock?

_____

_____

5. What does Jimmy do when he finds the rock?

_____

_____

6. Jimmy hides the rock in the pocket of an old jacket. Whom does the jacket belong to?

_____

_____

IV   Discussion
Look at the pictures. Talk to your partner. Use words from the story.

Picture #1.
Where is the bus driver?
Why does she have the paper bag?
What is she going to do?

Picture #2.
Why does Anna look sad?
Why does Peter have a curious expression on his face?

V   Writing

The rock goes to four different places in the story. What is the first place, and who are the people in this part of the story? What is the second place, the third, the fourth? Use words from the story.

_____

_____

_____

_____

_____

_____

"Is it really you?"

A Mother and a Mother-in-Law
A Comedy

THE CHARACTERS

Donna

June

Both women are about forty-five years old. They know each other from high school, but they are not close friends.

THE SCENE

A large supermarket

Donna is shopping for paper towels. June is shopping for paper napkins. Their shopping carts touch.

JUNE: Oh, pardon me! I'm sorry.

DONNA: That's all right. I can move my cart. *(She looks at June in surprise.)* June! Is it really you? I'm so glad to see you after so many years.

JUNE: Hello, Donna. You look very well.

DONNA: So do you. *(Each woman gives the other a little kiss on the cheek.)*

JUNE: How is your family? How is your daughter?

DONNA: Cathy? She is beautiful. She is such a lucky, lucky girl. Do you know she is married now?

JUNE: No. Congratulations. Who is her husband?

DONNA: His name is Rick. He's nice, but you understand, I'm her mother, and in my opinion, nobody is good enough for Cathy. *(She laughs to show that she is only joking.)*

JUNE: Is Cathy working?

DONNA: No, no. Not any more. Rick doesn't want his wife to work. He doesn't like her to clean the house or wash the dishes. He does most of that.

JUNE: Really? What does Cathy do all day?

DONNA: Well, Cathy needs a lot of rest, so she sleeps until noon. Then she gets dressed. She has so many pretty clothes. She meets her girl friends for lunch. After that, she goes shopping at the very best stores. She and Rick eat dinner in a restaurant two or three times a week. I tell you, Rick thinks Cathy is a queen. Of course, I am so happy for her.

JUNE: I can see that you are. Now I want to hear about your son. He's married, too, isn't he?

DONNA: Yes, David is married. Oh, June, my heart breaks for my son. He isn't lucky, like his sister, Cathy.

JUNE: What's the problem with David?

DONNA: The problem with David is David's wife, Patty. My daughter-in-law, Patty, is a good-for-nothing. She doesn't have a job anymore, and she doesn't even look for one. Patty is so lazy that she sleeps until noon. She leaves the dirty dishes in the sink while she goes out to eat lunch with her friends. Then she goes shopping and buys clothes she doesn't need. Two or three times a week, she and David eat dinner in a restaurant. Why? Because Patty doesn't like to cook, that's why. June, sometimes I want to cry. I feel so sorry for David.

JUNE: *(June looks unsympathetic.)* I do, too. I really do feel sorry for him. Well, I have to go now. Goodbye, Donna.

DONNA: Wait, June! Let's plan to see each other again next week. We can have a cup of coffee and talk some more.

June doesn't want to hear. She pushes her shopping cart away quickly.

Exercises

I   Vocabulary

You probably know many of these words from reading the story and looking at the pictures. If there are still some you don't know, look them up in your dictionary now.

towels	opinion	rest	touch
daughter-in-law	surprise	break	lucky
dirty	glad	enough	(un)sympathetic

II   Definitions

Try to guess the best definition for these words. Then look them up in your dictionary and draw a circle around the answer.

1. lucky
    a. having a good time
    b. having good fortune
    c. having good weather

2. opinion
    a. happiness
    b. joy
    c. judgment

3. dirty
    a. wise
    b. not wise
    c. not clean

4. enough
    a. dependably
    b. possibly
    c. sufficiently

5. (in) surprise
    a. (in) love
    b. (in) wonder
    c. (in) happiness

6. (un)sympathetic
    a. (not being) thirsty
    b. (not being) understanding
    c. (not being) helpful

III   Reading Comprehension

Read the questions. Find the answers in the story. Write the answers under the questions.

1. Donna says that nobody is good enough for Cathy. Then she laughs. Why does she laugh?

47

2. Why isn't Cathy working?

_____

_____

3. Why does Cathy sleep until noon?

_____

_____

4. Where does Cathy go shopping?

_____

_____

5. Why does Patty sleep until noon?

_____

_____

6. Why do Patty and David eat in a restaurant two or three times a week?

_____

_____

IV   Discussion

Look at the pictures. Talk to your partner. Use words from the story.

Picture #1.
Why is Donna so happy about her daughter, Cathy?
What does Cathy do all day?

Picture #2.
Why is Donna so sad about her son,
David?
Who is David's wife?
What does she do all day?

V   Writing

Why does Donna say her "heart breaks" for her son, David? Write three or four
reasons for his problems.

1. _____

2. _____

3. _____

4. _____

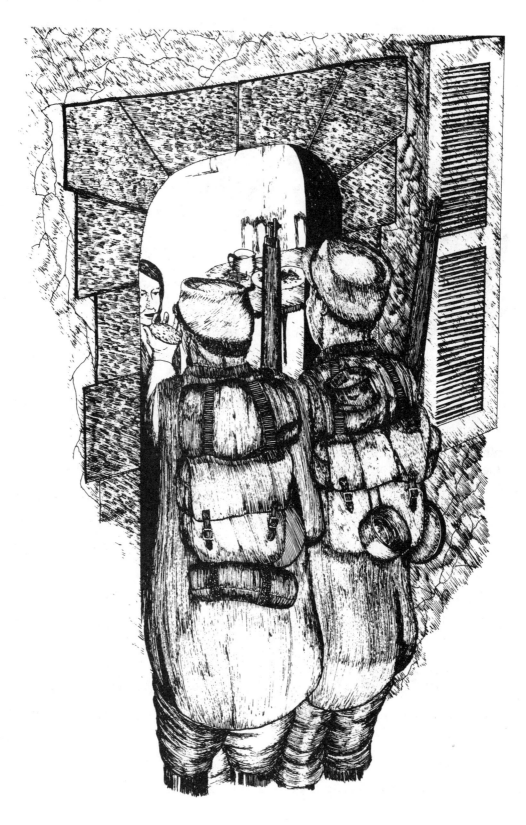

"With this stone, we can make delicious soup for the three of us."

Stone Soup
(An Old Folk Tale)

Two French soldiers are coming home from the war. They don't have horses to ride, so they walk. They walk a long, long way. They have little food and no money.

One of the soldiers is tall and thin. He is Leon. The other soldier is short and thin. He is Jules. By the time Leon and Jules come to a village, they have no more food. They are very hungry.

"Let's ask these good people for food," Jules says.

The soldiers do not know that the people in this village are selfish. They don't like to give anything to anyone.

Jules knocks at the door of a house. An old woman opens the door. Jules can see fresh bread on her table. There is butter and cheese, too.

"We are hungry," Jules tells the old woman. "Can you please give us something to eat?"

"I am a poor, old woman. I have nothing to give you," she says, and she closes the door.

Leon knocks on the door of another house. A fat man opens the door. Leon can see roast beef and vegetables on his table.

"Do you have a little food for two very hungry soldiers?" Leon asks.

"I am also poor," the fat man says. "There is no food in my house." He closes the door.

Leon looks at Jules. "These are not good people."

Jules tells Leon, "No, they are not. They are like pigs. They give nothing. They want to eat everything. But listen, friend. I have a plan to play a joke on these selfish people."

Jules whispers a secret into Leon's ear. Leon laughs.

"I like your plan," he says. "Let's do it."

Leon looks around for a small, flat stone. When he finds it, he puts it in his pocket. Then he and Jules knock on the door of a third house. A young woman opens the door. There is a dish of fried fish on her table. There is a cake and some milk.

"Can you please help two poor, hungry soldiers?" Leon asks.

"No," says the young woman. "I am as poor and hungry as you are."

Jules says, "I feel sad. Here we are, three people with nothing to eat. I am so sad that I want to cry."

"Don't cry, dear friend," Leon tells Jules. "Remember, we have my father's wonderful stone."

Leon takes the stone out of his pocket.

Jules says, "I am stupid! How can I forget your father's wonderful stone? With this stone, we can make delicious soup for the three of us."

The young woman wants to learn how to make soup from a stone. She is like the other selfish people in the village. She wants to keep everything for herself, and get something for nothing.

"My father's stone makes the best soup in the world," Leon tells her. "That is the truth. But I can't cook stone soup without a pot."

"You can take my pot," the young woman says.

The soldiers find some dry sticks to make a fire. Soon the pot of water is boiling, and Leon puts in the stone. Every ten minutes, Leon tastes it. All the villagers come to watch. One of them asks Leon how the soup tastes.

"Delicious," he says. "It needs an onion to make it even better. But, with or without an onion, stone soup is the best soup in the world."

The old woman is there, looking and listening. Her spoon is ready in her hand. She can't wait to eat that stone soup.

"I think I have an onion for the soup," she says. She runs home to get it.

Jules tastes the soup again. Leon tastes it again.

"How does the soup taste now?" the fat man asks.

"Delicious," Leon says. "It needs some potatoes and a piece of meat to make it even better. But, with or without potatoes, with or without meat, stone soup is the best soup in the world."

"I have potatoes," says one of the women.

"I have a piece of meat," says another.

In this way, Jules and Leon play their joke on the villagers. Someone brings carrots to make the soup even better. Others bring tomatoes, beans, rice, cabbage, salt and pepper. When the stone soup is ready to eat, it tastes good because it is full of good things. Everyone gets a little, but the soldiers eat and eat until they can eat no more.

"That soup really is the best soup in the world," the fat man tells the old woman.

"Yes," she says, "and it is made from only a stone! I want to have that stone."

All the women want it. All the men are thinking how to get it away from Leon.

One man says, "Hey, soldier! Give me the stone and these ten silver dollars are yours!"

"Sell it to me for twenty silver dollars," says another.

In the end, Leon sells the stone to the fat man for a hundred silver dollars. Then he and Jules walk down the road, laughing as hard as they can.

Exercises

I Vocabulary

You probably know many of these words from reading the story and looking at the pictures. If there are still some you don't know, look them up in your dictionary now

.

soldier	village	selfish	knock
hungry	plan	joke	whisper
secret	flat	cry	forget
stick	boil	taste	laugh

II Definitions

Try to guess the best definition for these words. Then look them up in your dictionary and draw a circle around the answer.

1. selfish
   - a. poor
   - b. educated
   - c. egoist

2. plan
   - a. a pocket
   - b. a plane
   - c. a project

3. joke
   - a. trick
   - b. game
   - c. trip

4. whisper
   - a. breathe
   - b. whistle loudly
   - c. talk quietly

5. secret
   - a. something private
   - b. something funny
   - c. something wise

6. forget
   - a. to eat with a fork
   - b. to remember
   - c. not to remember

III Reading Comprehension

Read the questions. Find the answers in the story. Write the answers under the questions.

1. Why are the two French soldiers walking?

   _____

   _____

2. What is it that Leon and Jules don't know about the people in the village?

   _____

   _____

3. What can Leon see on the fat man's table?

   _____

   _____

4. What does the young woman want to learn?

   _____

   _____

5. What does fat man tell the old woman?

   _____

   _____

6. What do Jules and Leon do after the fat man buys the stone for a hundred silver dollars?

   _____

   _____

IV   Discussion
Look at the pictures. Talk to your partner. Use words from the story.

Picture #1.
What is Leon and Jules' plan?
Why do they want to play a joke on
the people of the village?

Picture #2.
What do Jules and Leon put in the
pot?
What do the villagers bring to them?
Why is the soup delicious?

V   Writing

Write two things you know about the people of the village.

1. _____

2. _____

Write one reason why the people of the village want the stone.

1. _____

"There! Is that what you want?"

Jack and the Bandit
A Comedy

THE CHARACTERS
Jack Jones
A Bandit

THE SCENE
A dark forest. It is a cold, winter night. Jack Jones is walking home from the city. As he walks, he whistles a happy Christmas song. Suddenly a bandit jumps out from behind a tree. He is holding a gun.

BANDIT: Give me your money. Quick!

JACK: Don't shoot! Please don't shoot!

BANDIT: Give me your money or you are going to die. I mean what I say!

JACK: *(He takes his money out of his pocket and hands it to the bandit.)* Five months. That's how long I have to work to get this much money. I work very hard. I am on my way home from the city where I work. I want to buy my wife a warm coat. I want to buy my children shoes and toys for Christmas. Now I don't have money to buy anything.

BANDIT: *(He is counting the money.)* That's your problem. That's not my problem.

JACK: My wife is not going to believe me when I tell her that a bandit in the forest has all our Christmas money.

BANDIT: *(He puts the money in his pocket.)* Your wife is your problem. She's not my problem.

JACK: I understand that. But if you want to help me a little, there is something you can do. You can make my wife believe me when I tell her that a bandit has our money.

BANDIT: How can I do that?

JACK: Shoot a bullet into my hat. When my wife sees the bullet hole, she is going to understand right away what a dangerous man you are.

BANDIT: *(He laughs. He likes the idea. He wants people to think he is a dangerous man. He pulls Jack's hat off, throws it into the air, and shoots at it.)* There! Is that what you want?

JACK: Thank you. That's exactly right. *(He takes off his jacket.)* Now shoot a hole in my jacket, please. *(The bandit shoots a hole in Jack's jacket.)* Thank you. That's exactly right. *(Jack takes off his shirt.)* Now shoot a hole in my shirt, please.

BANDIT: I can't. I have no more bullets.

JACK: Oh, so you have no more bullets. Friend, that's your problem. That's not my problem. *(Jack pushes the bandit down. He hits and kicks him. He takes all the money back. The bandit runs away. Jacks puts his clothes on again, and puts his money back in his pocket. He starts walking home again. As he walks, he whistles a happy Christmas song.)*

Exercises

I   Vocabulary

You probably know many of these words from reading the story and looking at the pictures. If there are still some you don't know, look them up in your dictionary now.

character	bandit	scene	whistle
suddenly	shoot	die	believe
bullet	idea	throw	hole
push	pull	hit	kick

II   Definitions

Try to guess the best definition for these words. Then look them up in your dictionary and draw a circle around the answer.

1. character
   a. a thing to see
   b. a place in a city
   c. a person in a story

2. bandit
   a. enemy
   b. musician
   c. criminal

3. suddenly
   a. slowly
   b. strongly
   c. quickly

4. believe
   a. to think
   b. to teach
   c. to pretend

5. idea
   a. a thread
   b. a thumb
   c. a thought

6. hit
   a. to step
   b. to stop
   c. to strike

III   Reading Comprehension

Read the questions. Find the answers in the story. Write the answers under the questions.

1. What happens to Jack Jones when he is walking home from the city?

   _____

   _____

61

2. What does Jack do with his money?

    _____

    _____

3. What does Jack say he wants to buy for his wife?

    _____

    _____

4. What does the bandit want people to think?

    _____

    _____

5. What does the bandit do to Jack's jacket?

    _____

    _____

6. What does the bandit say when Jack asks him to shoot a hole in his shirt?

    _____

    _____

IV   Discussion
Look at the pictures. Talk to your partner. Use words from the story.

Picture #1.
What is Jack doing in the forest?
Who is behind the tree?
Is he a dangerous man?
Why?

Picture #2.
What does Jack want the bandit to do?
Why?
Does the bandit shoot Jack's jacket?
Why?

V   Writing

Dictation. Study the last paragraph in the story beginning with JACK: "Oh, so you have no more bullets." Close your book as the teacher dictates. Then open your book and check your work.

_____

_____

_____

_____

_____

_____

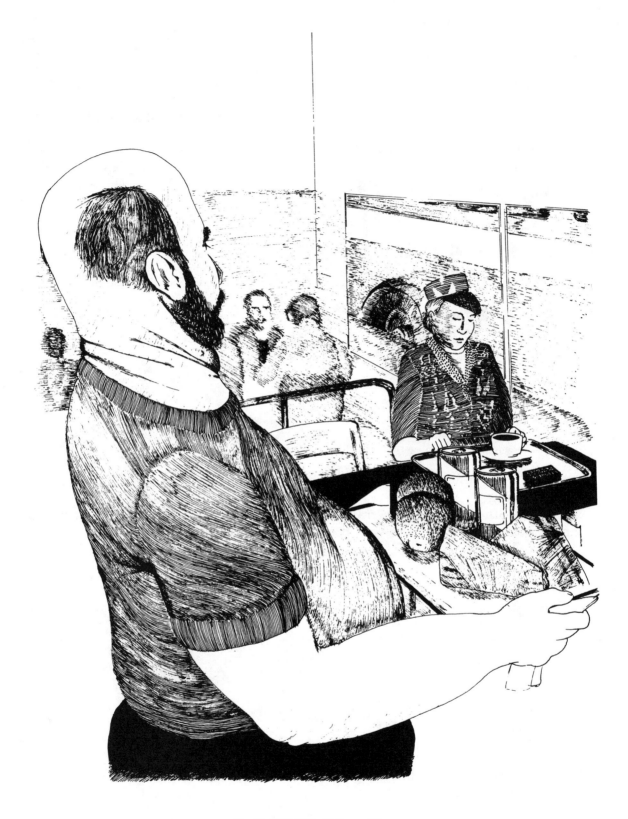

"Is it OK if I sit here?"

A Box of Chocolates

Mrs. Helen Gray is going to New York City. She is going to see her first grand-daughter. Helen is riding the bus from Houston, Texas, to New York, New York. She prefers to fly, but the bus is more economical.

The bus ride is long, but there are interesting things to see. The bus stops in many cities. The passengers get off to buy food in the bus stations. Most of the time, Helen buys a sandwich and a cup of coffee. She always buys picture post cards to send to her friends in Houston.

Today the bus driver says, "We are coming into Chicago, Illinois. We're staying there one hour. If anyone is hungry, there is a restaurant in the station."

Helen is very hungry. She buys a chicken sandwich and an orange and coffee. Then she buys a small box of chocolate candy from a candy machine. These candies are called Hershey's Kisses. Helen likes them.

Helen sits at a table and eats her lunch. There are too many people in the restaurant. A man comes to Helen's table. He is a very big man. He has two sandwiches, two oranges, and two soft drinks but he has no place to sit.

He asks Helen, "Is it OK if I sit here?"

"Yes, it's OK," she says. But she is thinking, "Oh, why don't you sit at another table? I don't like your face or your expression. You don't look like a good person. You look like a criminal."

The man eats his sandwiches. He doesn't look at Helen. She doesn't look at him. She remembers that she wants to buy picture post cards, and goes to get them. When she comes back the big man is eating a chocolate out of a little box of Hershey's Kisses.

Helen is furious. He is eating her candy. She wants to say something to him, but she is afraid. He is so big and she is so small. She is VERY angry, though, so she takes the box of candy away from him, removes the silver paper from one candy, and puts it in her mouth. The man looks at Helen. He is surprised. Then he pulls the box from her, eats the last candy, and throws the box away. He stands up.

"Lady," he says, "I think you are sick. I think you are mentally sick."

He walks away.

Helen is still very angry when it is time to get on the bus. She thinks, "I'm right. That man is a criminal. I think he is mentally sick, and he looks dangerous."

She opens her purse to look at the post cards. There, under the cards, is a little box of Hershey's Kisses.

Exercises

I Vocabulary

You probably know many of these words from reading the story and looking at the pictures. If there are still some you don't know, look them up in your dictionary now.

candy	chicken	criminal	dangerous	
economical	furious	granddaughter	interesting	
machine	mental(ly)	passenger	post card	
prefer	sick	soft drink	station	afraid

II Definitions

Try to guess the best definition for these words. Then look them up in your dictionary and draw a circle around the answer.

1. granddaughter
   a. her mother's mother
   b. her daughter's mother
   c. her son's daughter

2. prefer
   a. to agree with
   b. to like more
   c. to try harder

3. economical
   a. to cost more money
   b. to cost the same
   c. to cost less money

4. mental(ly)
   a. in the middle
   b. on the menu
   c. in the mind

5. soft drink
   a. milk
   b. tea
   c. soda

6. furious
   a. very happy
   b. very angry
   c. very hungry

III Reading Comprehension

Read the questions. Find the answers in the story. Write the answers under the questions.

1. Why is Helen going to New York?

_____

_____

2. Why isn't she flying?

_____

_____

3. Why does Helen always buy picture post cards?

_____

_____

4. What does Helen buy from a candy machine?

_____

_____

5. Why does the big man ask Helen if he can sit at her table?

_____

_____

6. What does the big man do with the box after he eats the last candy?

_____

_____

IV Discussion
Look at the pictures. Talk to your partner. Use words from the story.

Picture #1.
Who are these people?
What are they doing?
What is she thinking?

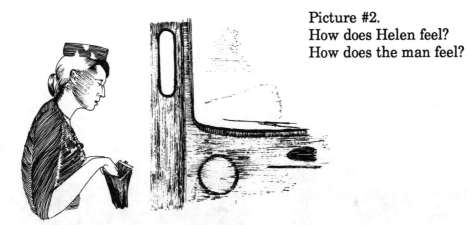

Picture #2.
How does Helen feel?
How does the man feel?

V Writing

Dictation. Study the second paragraph in the story for a few minutes. Think about spelling and punctuation. Then close your book and write as the teacher dictates. When you finish, open your book and check your work. Correct your mistakes.

_____

_____

_____

_____

_____

The other two do what the driver asks, but Rosa does not.

Rosa Parks Goes to Jail

It is a cold evening near Christmas time, 1955, in the city of Montgomery, Alabama. Rosa Parks, a black woman, is leaving the department store where she works hard at a sewing machine every day. The store is very busy at this holiday time, and tonight Rosa feels especially tired. She usually walks home, but tonight she decides to take the bus. This simple decision changes not only her life, but the lives of most black people in the United States.

The bus company in Montgomery makes black people sit at the back of their buses. Some bus drivers make the blacks come in at the front of the bus to pay and then go out again and enter through the back door of the bus to sit. Rosa hates this.

Finally the bus arrives, and she is glad to see that there is an empty seat in the first row of the section for the blacks. Rosa sits next to two blacks in this row, and the bus starts again. Soon the bus is full of passengers. The last one is a white man, and there are no more empty seats. The bus driver looks at the row where Rosa is sitting, and tells her and the other two to go and stand at the very back of the bus. The other two do what the driver asks, but Rosa does not. Something deep in her heart makes her resist giving her seat to a man only because he is white. She suddenly feels very brave.

"Are you getting up?" the driver asks her.

"No, I am not," Rosa answers quietly.

"Then I have to call the police," the driver says.

"Call them," Rosa tells him.

The police come and take Rosa to jail. She is there until her husband and a lawyer come with money to get her out. A few days later, Rosa goes to court. The judge says she is guilty of breaking the law. In many states in the south the law requires segregation of blacks in public places. Rosa Parks and her lawyer decide to take this case to a higher court. They want to take it all the way to the Supreme Court of the United States.

The whole black community learns of Rosa's arrest. When important things happen, the people usually go to their churches to be together and to hear what their ministers say. The church where Mr. and Mrs. Parks go has a new young minister whose name is Dr. Martin Luther King, Jr. No one, at this time, knows very much about him. Dr. King and the other black ministers ask everyone to boycott the buses, not to ride in them until the bus company accepts that the Constitution of the United States gives black people equal rights with white people. This is the beginning of the great Montgomery bus boycott, which continues for 381 days. Dr. King is its leader, and he is soon famous all over the world.

For 381 difficult days almost every black person walks to work or school. Old and young, fathers, mothers and children get up early in the morning so they can arrive on time. The bus company begins to lose hundreds of thousands of dollars because so many people are not riding on the buses. Rosa loses her job because she works for the boycott. She goes to many other cities to speak to people and tell them what is happening in Montgomery. The whole nation watches the boycott on T.V. Black people everywhere begin to demand equal rights.

Finally, the Supreme Court gives the decision everyone is waiting for. It says that people of any color can sit where they want on any bus, train or plane.

It is a great victory, not only for Rosa Parks and the black community of Montgomery, but for all the people of the United States. Most important, it is a victory for the United States Constitution, which promises equal rights and equal justice to everyone.

NOTE: boycott — to refuse to buy, sell or use (something)

Exercises

I Vocabulary

You probably know many of these words from reading the story and looking at the pictures. If there are still some you don't know, look them up in your dictionary now.

sewing machine	busy	passenger	deep	court
heart	brave	quiet	jail	
lawyer	judge	guilty	segregation	
minister	boycott	rights	victory	
constitution	justice	require	community	

II Definitions

Try to guess the best definition for these words. Then look them up in your dictionary and draw a circle around the answer.

1. brave
   a. courteous
   b. courageous
   c. feverish

2. (is) guilty
   a. has blame
   b. has courage
   c. is hungry

3. segregation
   a. examination
   b. demonstration
   c. separation

4. minister
   a. a good boss
   b. a religious leader
   c. a brave person

5. boycott
   a. not to sell or give
   b. not to tell or answer
   c. not to use or buy

6. rights
   a. money
   b. happiness
   c. privileges

III Reading Comprehension

Read the questions. Find the answers in the story. Write the answers under the questions.

1. Why does Rosa decide to take the bus home from work?

2. Where does the bus company in Montgomery make black people sit?

_____

_____

3. What does Rosa say when the bus driver asks her if she is getting up?

_____

_____

4. What is the name of the new young minister in the church where Rosa and her husband go?

_____

_____

5. Why does Rosa lose her job?

_____

_____

6. What does the United States Constitution promise?

_____

_____

IV Discussion

Look at the pictures. Talk to your partner. Use words from the story.

Picture #1.
Who is the minister?
What is he asking
everyone to do?

74

Picture #2.
What is the decision of the
Supreme Court?
Why is it important?

V   Writing

Dictation. Study the last paragraph in the story beginning with "It is a great
victory..." As you write, be careful of punctuation. Close your book as the teacher
dictates. Then open your book and check your work.

_____

_____

_____

_____

It is not easy to live in a small house with a horse, a goat, eight chickens, seven children and a wife who doesn't talk to you.

The Rabbi and the Shoemaker

(An Old Folk Tale)

Far away, in another country, there is a small village. In this village, there is a poor shoemaker. His name is Jacob. He lives in a house that has only two rooms. One of these rooms is where Jacob works. All day he puts new soles and new heels on old shoes.

Jacob has a wife, Isobel, and seven small children. In the summer, life is not bad. The babies sleep under the trees and the older children play in the sun. But summer is short and winter is long. In the winter, the children stay in the house to keep warm. The babies cry day and night. The older children run around and around, from one room to the other. They play. They jump. They fall. They shout at each other. Isobel shouts at them. Jacob shouts at her. In the winter, life is not good.

Jacob thinks, "This house is too small. We need a bigger house. But I am a poor man. What can I do?"

In the village where Jacob lives there is a famous rabbi. Everyone says this rabbi is wise and wonderful. People who have problems go to him for help. Jacob thinks, "Maybe the rabbi can help me, too."

The rabbi is very old. He has a white beard. All day, every day, he reads and studies big books that are older than he is. But he is a good man, so he takes off his reading glasses and listens when Jacob comes to explain his problem.

"I see," says the rabbi. "Your house is too small. But why are you telling me? Am I a carpenter? Do you think I can make your house bigger?"

"I don't know, Rabbi," Jacob says sadly. "Maybe that is impossible."

"Nothing is impossible," the rabbi says. "I can try. But you have to promise to do anything I ask."

"I promise, I promise," says Jacob.

"Good. Do you have a cow? Do you have chickens?"

Jacob says he has a goat and eight chickens.

NOTE: A rabbi is a religious leader and a teacher of Jewish law.

"Take the goat and the chickens into the house," the rabbi tells him. "Keep them there ten days. Then come back and tell me if the house is bigger."

"Rabbi," Jacob says, "you don't understand. There isn't room for a mouse in my house...."

But the rabbi puts his reading glasses on again. When his glasses are on, he can't hear anything. Jacob walks home. He feels worse than before.

A promise is a promise. Jacob takes the animals into the house. Isobel gets very angry. She doesn't talk to Jacob. Now the house is more uncomfortable than ever. It smells terrible. There are chicken feathers everywhere. Ten days go by slowly.

On the eleventh day, Jacob tells the rabbi that the house seems smaller than before. The rabbi pulls his white beard and thinks. He asks Jacob, "Do you have any other animals?"

"A horse," answers Jacob.

"Take the horse into your house. Keep him there ten days. Then come back and tell me if your house is bigger."

"Rabbi, I can't do that! My wife hates me already!"

But the rabbi puts on his glasses and can't hear a word.

It is not easy to live in a small house with a horse, a goat, eight chickens, seven children and a wife who doesn't talk to you. Ten days go by very, very slowly.

On the eleventh day. Jacob comes to the rabbi. He is too unhappy to speak. The rabbi takes off his glasses. "Jacob," he says, "this is the day. I know it. Take all the animals out. Your house is bigger. I can see it from here. Go home and you can see it, too."

Jacob runs home. He opens the door and lets the animals out. Without the animals, the house is now comfortable. Without the animals, the house seems very big.

"Yes, it is bigger," Jacob tells Isobel, who now talks to him. "I think it's much bigger."

Isobel smiles. "Our rabbi is truly a wise and wonderful man," she says.

Exercises

I Vocabulary

You probably know many of these words from reading the story and looking at the pictures. If there are still some you don't know, look them up in your dictionary now.

far	village	shoe	heel
jump	shout	wise	wonderful
beard	carpenter	feather	hate
unhappy	comfortable	worse	sole

II Definitions

Try to guess the best definition for these words. Then look them up in your dictionary and draw a circle around the answer.

1. shout (at)
   a. smile at
   b. cry out
   c. speak

2. wise
   a. old
   b. kind
   c. knowing

3. wonderful
   a. ordinary
   b. extraordinary
   c. average

4. hate
   a. discover
   b. discuss
   c. dislike

5. unhappy
   a. sincere
   b. selfish
   c. sad

6. comfortable
   a. complete
   b. convenient
   c. confident

III Reading Comprehension

Read the questions. Find the answers in the story. Write the answers under the questions.

1. What do Jacob's babies do in the summer?

_____

_____

79

2. What do they do in the winter?

_____

_____

3. What does everyone say about the famous rabbi who lives in the village?

_____

_____

4. What does the rabbi hear when he puts his reading glasses on?

_____

_____

5. What does Isobel do when she gets very angry?

_____

_____

6. How does the house smell after Jacob takes all the animals in?

_____

_____

IV Discussion
Look at the pictures. Talk to your partner. Use words from the story.

Picture #1.
Who is this old man?
What is he reading?
What do people say about him?
Why do people go to him?

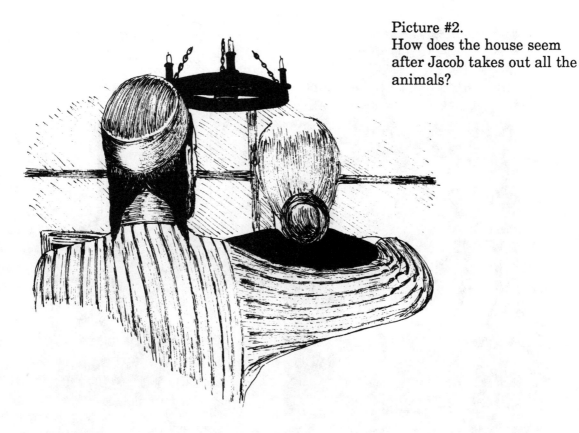

Picture #2.
How does the house seem
after Jacob takes out all the
animals?

V   Writing
Write three things to describe the rabbi.

1. _____

2. _____

3. _____

Write three things to describe life in the winter at Jacob's house.

1. _____

2. _____

3. _____

"There is enough pizza for both of us."

My Lucky Apartment

Steven Kay is putting a pizza in his oven for dinner. He is in his new apartment, and he feels especially happy.

"I am lucky," Steve thinks. "I have a new job in a new city, and now I have a new apartment, too. Not many young men who are my age have such a nice place to live."

Steve can't understand why Carl, who owns the building, rents the apartment for so little money.

"Some day I am going to ask Carl about that," Steve thinks. Then he tells himself, "No, I'm not going to ask him that question. I don't want him to raise the rent."

Steve's pizza is hot now. He sits down to eat it, but just then the doorbell rings.

"I wonder who that is?," Steve thinks.

It is a girl, a very pretty girl. Steve does not know her. It is October, and the weather is cold, but she is wearing a blue summer dress and a white summer hat. She smiles at Steve.

"Please come in," Steve tells her.

"Thank you. My name is Gloria Lee," she says. "I like the way my apartment looks. It is just the way I remember it."

"*Your* apartment?" Steve asks.

Gloria smiles. "I know, I know, it is not my apartment any more. But I still like it. I am sad that I have to live — in another place."

Gloria walks around the apartment, looking at everything. She takes off her hat and puts it on a chair. Now Steve can see her face better. She is beautiful. Her hair is long and dark. Her eyes are dark, too, as dark as night.

"Are you looking for something?" Steve asks her. "There is a red jacket in the closet. Is it yours?"

"Oh, it probably is," Gloria answers, "but I don't want it. I don't need it any more. No, I just want to see my old apartment one more time. Thanks for letting me in. Now I am leaving and you can eat your dinner before it gets cold."

Steve does not want Gloria to go. He is a young man who is very interested in beautiful young women, and this one is more beautiful and more mysterious than any girl he knows.

"There is enough pizza for both of us," he says.

"Thank you," Gloria tells him, "but I have to leave."

"Wait!" Steve says. "Maybe we can meet again. Please, give me your telephone number so I can call you."

Gloria opens the door. "I'm sorry, I don't have a telephone."

Then she is gone.

As Steve starts to eat dinner, he thinks about Gloria. He wants to see her again. He wonders if Carl knows where she lives now. Carl has an apartment in the same building. Steve leaves his pizza on the table, goes up to Carl's apartment, and rings the doorbell. He tells Carl about Gloria's visit.

"Carl," Steve says, "Gloria is the most interesting and the most beautiful girl in the world. Do you know her very well? Can you tell me where she lives now?"

As he listens to Steve, Carl's eyes get big. Steve can see that he is afraid of something.

Carl says, "Steve, you don't know what you are talking about!"

Carl shows Steve an old newspaper. The date is June 6 last year. The newspaper says, "GIRL KILLED — KILLER GETS AWAY." There is a picture of Gloria in the same blue summer dress. She lies dead on the kitchen floor of the apartment.

"So that's why the rent is so low," Steve says.

"Yes." Carl answers, "People don't want to live in that apartment. Listen, Steve, now do you understand that what you tell me is impossible? Gloria cannot visit you. She is dead!"

Steve goes back to his apartment. He is confused.

"I don't understand," he thinks. "I know one thing. I don't believe in spirits. Can Gloria's visit be only my imagination? Yes, Steve decides, "It is just my imagination. Gloria is just a dream."

He sits down at the table again, to eat his pizza. There, on the chair, is Gloria's white summer hat.

Exercises

I   Vocabulary

You probably know many of these words from reading the story and looking at the pictures. If there are still some you don't know, look them up in your dictionary now.

especially	job	raise	weather	gone
remember	interested	mysterious	afraid	doorbell
confused	spirits	dream	imagination	

II   Definitions

Try to guess the best definition for these words. Then look them up in your dictionary and draw a circle around the answer.

1. especially
   - a. mostly
   - b. particularly
   - c. nearly

2. raise
   - a. make lower
   - b. make equal
   - c. make higher

3. mysterious
   - a. open
   - b. closed
   - c. secret

4. confused
   - a. puzzled
   - b. hungry
   - c. unhappy

5. spirit
   - a. fire
   - b. fight
   - c. phantom

6. imagination
   - a. fact
   - b. fortune
   - c. fantasy

III   Reading Comprehension

Read the questions. Find the answers in the story. Write the answers under the questions.

1. What is Gloria wearing when she rings Steve's doorbell?

_____

_____

2. Why doesn't Steve want Gloria to go?

_____

_____

3. What does Gloria say when Steve asks her for her telephone number?

_____

_____

4. Where does Carl live?

_____

_____

5. What does Carl show Steve?

_____

_____

6. What does Steve find on the chair?

_____

_____

IV Discussion
Look at the pictures. Talk to your partner. Use words from the story.

Picture #1.
What is Steve doing?
Why is he smiling?
Why does he feel lucky?

Picture #2.
What is Carl showing Steve?
What does Carl tell Steve?
What question does Carl answer for Steve?

V Writing

Write three things you know about Gloria from the story.

1. _____

2. _____

3. _____

Write two reasons you think Steve is lucky.

1. _____

2. _____

Write one reason why you do or do not think Gloria is just a dream.

1. _____

"Why is this parrot so expensive?" Leonard wants to know.

Maybe Some Parrots Need to Speak Better English

Leonard Longfellow loves his mother. He telephones her at home in Los Angeles twice a week. Leonard is a very rich business man who travels often, and his telephone calls sometimes come from London, or Tokyo, or Buenos Aires, or Moscow, or any important city.

In addition to calling his mother twice a week, Leonard gives her beautiful presents. When he is away from home because he is traveling, he sends her beautiful presents—for her birthday, for Christmas, and especially for Mother's Day. Now it is almost Mother's Day, and Leonard is in Paris, France.

He wonders what to buy for Mother's Day this year. He sees large bottles of expensive perfume in a department store window.

"No, not perfume again," he thinks. "Mother has enough perfume."

He stops to look at some nice gold bracelets in another store window.

"No," he says, "not gold bracelets again. Mother has enough gold bracelets."

He looks at rings, he looks at necklaces, but he doesn't find anything that is just right for his mother.

Then Leonard goes around a corner and walks on a different street. He comes to a pet store. There are two pretty kittens in the window.

"No, not kittens," Leonard thinks. "Mother doesn't like kittens because they grow up to be cats, and cats catch birds. Birds... BIRDS! What a good idea! I'm going to buy mother a bird, a bird that can talk to her when she is alone."

Leonard tells the man who works in the store that he wants to buy a parrot. There are four parrots in the store. All four are bright green and red and yellow, and they are speaking French in loud, disagreeable voices. Three of the parrots cost two hundred dollars. The fourth one costs five hundred dollars.

"Why is this parrot so expensive?" Leonard wants to know.

"Because this bird has great intelligence," the man explains. "He speaks seven languages. The other three speak only French."

Leonard pays five hundred dollars for the intelligent parrot that speaks French, Spanish, Japanese, Russian, Hebrew, Portuguese and English. He is especially happy that it speaks English, which is the only language his mother understands. He pays almost a hundred dollars more to send the bird to Los Angeles by air express.

On Mother's Day, Leonard telephones his mother from Paris.

"Happy Mother's Day, Mama," he tells her.

"Thank you," she answers. "You're such a good son to remember your mother."

"Is my present there yet?" Leonard asks.

"Yes, of course, it's here," his mother says.

"Do you like it?"

"Do I like it? I *love* it! It's on the table here in front of me right now. Let me tell you something, Leonard. With a few tomatoes and some rice it's absolutely *delicious!*"

"Delicious?" says Leonard, "Mama, are you eating the talking parrot that speaks seven languages?"

"Seven languages!" his mother answers. "Well, son, maybe some parrots need to speak better English!"

Exercises

I   Vocabulary
You probably know many of these words from reading the story and looking at the pictures. If there are still some you don't know, look them up in your dictionary now.

travel	birthday	cat	kitten
catch	loud	bracelet	disagreeable
ring	necklace	pet	(in) addition (to)
especially	idea	intelligence	

II   Definitions
Try to guess the best definition for these words. Then look them up in your dictionary and draw a circle around the answer.

1. catch
   - a. cut
   - b. capture
   - c. cover

2. pet
   - a. a cow
   - b. a dog
   - c. a chicken

3. disagreeable (voice)
   - a. a low voice
   - b. an unpleasant voice
   - c. a soft voice

4. loud (voice)
   - a. strong
   - b. quiet
   - c. delicate

5. (in) addition (to)
   - a. sometimes
   - b. also
   - c. never

6. intelligence
   - a. happiness
   - b. health
   - c. understanding

III   Reading Comprehension
Read the questions. Find the answers in the story. Write the answers under the questions.

1. How often does Leonard telephone his mother?

   _____

   _____

91

2. What does Leonard send his mother?

_____

_____

3. Why doesn't Leonard want to buy gold bracelets?

_____

_____

4. Why doesn't Leonard's mother like kittens?

_____

_____

5. Why is the parrot Leonard buys more expensive than the other parrots?

_____

_____

6. What is the only language Mama understands?

_____

_____

IV   Discussion
Look at the pictures. Talk to your partner. Use words from the story.

Picture #1.
Why is Leonard in
front of the store
window?
What is he
thinking about
the things he
sees?

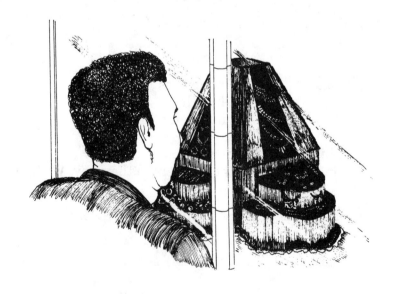

Picture #2.
Who is calling Mother?
What day is it?
Why does Mother's face have such an
expression of surprise?

V Writing

Dictation. Study the last paragraph in the story beginning with "On Mother's Day
Leonard telephones her from Paris." As you write, be careful about punctuation.
Close your book as the teacher dictates. Then open your book and check your work.

Up, up, up! Apollo 11 is up and away!

Launching the Apollo 11 — The First Journey to the Moon

On July 20, 1969, a dream that is thousands of years old comes true. For the first time a man from earth walks on the moon. His name is Neil A. Armstrong, and he is the commander of the spaceship Apollo 11. The two astronauts who fly to the moon with Armstrong are Edwin E. Aldrin and Michael Collins.

Preparations for this great adventure into space begin in 1961 when President John F. Kennedy decides that the United States is going to send a man to the moon and bring him back safely to earth.

Before that can happen, there is much work to do and there are many difficult questions to answer. The moon is very far away from the earth. Can we build a spaceship with enough power to get there? There is no air to breathe on the moon, and no water to drink. Daytime temperatures are unbelievably hot, and nighttime temperatures are unbelievably cold. Can we find a way for our astronauts to live in such temperatures, without air or water?

Scientists work together to make a journey to the moon possible. Some of them make space suits to protect the astronauts from the moon's temperature. Others find a way to give the astronauts air and water through their space suits. They build a rocket with so much power that it can lift the heavy spaceship away from the earth and start it on its journey to the moon.

All this takes time. Eight years pass. It is sad that President Kennedy does not live to see the launching of Apollo 11 on July 16, 1969. A million people come to watch the launching of the great rocket. Millions more see it on television. Early in the morning, before it is light, Armstrong, Aldrin and Collins, wearing their space suits, go into the spaceship. Preparations continue. Everyone is nervous. The countdown begins: five, four, three, two, one…ZERO.

Up, up, up! Apollo 11 is up and away! The launch is perfect. Everything is working perfectly. Apollo 11 is going to the moon at a speed of 24,000 miles an hour.

Four days after the launching, when they are very near the moon, Armstrong and Aldrin leave the spaceship. They are going to go the rest of the way in a small machine they call the Eagle. Collins stays in the Apollo. He flies around and around the moon, waiting to take the others back to earth.

Now the world holds its breath, as the Eagle slowly comes down on the surface of the moon. Armstrong's heart, which usually beats 77 times a minute, is beating 156 times a minute as the Eagle touches the moon.

Everywhere, in every country, wherever there is television, people are watching as Armstrong comes out of the Eagle and takes the first step on the surface of the moon.

He tells the world, "That's one small step for a man, and one giant leap for mankind."

Nineteen minutes later, Aldrin leaves the Eagle and meets with Armstrong on the moon. For the next 2 hours they take photographs and do scientific experiments. Together, they place an American flag in the moon's gray surface, where it stands to this day.

On July 24, after eight days in space, all three astronauts return safely to earth.

Exercises

I   Vocabulary

You probably know many of these words from reading the story and looking at the pictures. If there are still some you don't know, look them up in your dictionary now.

dream	commander	preparation	temperature	decide
scientist	astronaut	launch	speed	
beat	step	giant leap	mankind	
experiment	surface	rocket	space	

II   Definitions

Try to guess the best definition for these words. Then look them up in your dictionary and draw a circle around the answer.

1. dream
   a. an insult
   b. an instant
   c. an idea

2. launch
   a. start
   b. stop
   c. stay

3. speed
   a. victory
   b. velocity
   c. value

4. giant leap
   a. foolish joke
   b. enormous jump
   c. interesting journey

5. experiment
   a. test
   b. thing
   c. thought

6. surface
   a. open
   b. only
   c. outside

III   Reading Comprehension

Read the questions. Find the answers in the story. Write the answers under the questions.

1. Who is Neil Armstrong?

_____

_____

2. What does President Kennedy decide?

_____

_____

3. What do scientists work together to do?

_____

_____

4. At what speed is Apollo 11 going to the moon?

_____

_____

5. What is astronaut Collins doing while Armstrong and Aldrin are walking on the moon?

_____

_____

6. What happens on July 24, 1969, after eight days in space?

_____

_____

IV   Discussion

Look at the pictures. Talk to your partner. Use words from the story.

Picture #1.
What do scientists need to do to make
a journey to the moon possible?

98

Picture #2.
How long do the astronauts stay on the moon?
What do they do?

V   Writing
Dictation. Study the fourth paragraph in the story, beginning with "Scientists work together..." As you write, be careful about punctuation. Close your book as the teacher dictates. Then open your book and check your work.

_____

_____

_____

_____

_____

WORD LIST

This comprehensive word list includes vocabulary from the stories which might be new to some advanced primary level students. Cognates of Spanish are here marked "C." Words found in the *Oxford Picture Dictionary of American English* are marked "O." Those found in Robert J. Dixson's *The 2,000 Most Frequently Used Words In English* are marked "D."

A

absolutely	C		D
accept	C		D
addition	C		D
afraid			D
age			D
almost			D
alone			D
angry			D
apartment	C	O	D
ashamed			D
astronaut	C	O	

B

bag		O	D
bandit	C		
bean		O	D
beard		O	D
beat		O	D
believe			D
bell		O	D
belong			D
bench		O	
binoculars	C		
bird		O	D
birthday		O	D
bite			D
boil		O	D
book		O	
both			D
bottle	C	O	D
box		O	D
bracelet	C	O	

bread		O	D
break		O	D
breath			D
breathe			D
bright			D
bring			D
bullet	C	O	D
bus	C	O	D
business			D
butter			D

C

cabbage		O	
cake		O	D
camera	C	O	D
candy			D
card(s)		O	D
carpenter	C	O	D
carrot		O	
cat		O	D
catch		O	D
character	C		D
cheek		O	
cheese		O	D
chicken		O	D
chocolate	C		
city		O	D
close			D
closet		O	
coat		O	D
coffee	C	O	D
comedy	C		
comfortable	C		D

Word	C	O	D
command			D
commander	C		
community	C		
complain			D
confuse	C		D
congratulations	C		D
constitution	C		
count	C		D
country		O	D
court		O	D
cow			D
crime			D
criminal	C		D
cross	C		D
crutch		O	
cry		O	D
curious	C		D

D

dangerous			D
dark		O	D
daughter-in-law		O	
dead			D
decide	C		D
deep			D
delicious	C		D
department	C	O	D
dial		O	
die			D
difficult	C		D
dirty		O	D
disagreeable	C		D
doctor	C	O	D
donkey		O	
dream		O	D
drive(r)		O	D
dry		O	D

E

eagle		O	
earth		O	D
economical	C		
elevator	C		D
empty		O	D
enough			D
especially	C		D
examination	C		D
excited	C		D
excuse			D
expensive			D
experiment	C		D
expression	C		D

F

family	C	O	D
far			D
farmer			D
feathers			D
feet		O	
fence		O	D
finally	C		D
find			D
fish		O	D
flat			D
follow			D
fool			D
foolish			D
foot		O	D
forest		O	D
friend			D
furious	C		

G

giant			
glad			D
glass		O	D
glasses		O	
goat		O	
gold			D
gone			D

Word	C	O	D
granddaughter		O	
grow			D
gun		O	D

H
Word	C	O	D
hammer		O	
hand		O	D
hang			D
happy		O	D
hard		O	D
hate			D
head		O	D
heart		O	D
heel		O	
hero	C		D
hide			D
hit		O	D
hit(ting)			D
hole			D
horse		O	D
hour		O	D
hungry			D
hurt			D
husband		O	D

I
Word	C	O	D
idea	C		D
imagination	C		D
imagine	C		D
important	C		D
intelligence	C		D
interesting	C		D

J
Word	C	O	D
jacket	C	O	
jail		O	
job			D
joke			D

K
Word	C	O	D
kick			D
kill			D
kill(er)			D
kiss		O	D
kitten		O	
knock			D

L
Word	C	O	D
ladder		O	D
language	C		D
laugh		O	D
launch		O	
lazy			D
leap		O	
license	C	O	
like			D
lonely			D
loud			D
lucky			D

M
Word	C	O	D
machine	C		D
man(kind)		O	D
marry			D
meat		O	D
mental(ly)	C		
milk		O	D
month		O	D
moon		O	D
mouse		O	D
move	C		D
murder			D
mysterious	C		D

N
Word	C	O	D
neck		O	D
necklace		O	
neighbor			D
nervous	C		D
newspaper		O	D
nice			D
number		O	D

	C	O	D
O			
obsidian	C		
office	C	O	D
old		O	D
old(er)			D
onion		O	D
opinion	C		D
orange		O	D
oven		O	D
P			
pain	C		D
paint(er)	C	O	D
palm	C	O	
pardon	C		D
park	C	O	D
parrot		O	
passenger	C	O	D
perfume	C	O	
pet			D
plan	C		D
plate	C	O	D
pocket		O	D
pole		O	
polite			D
poor			D
postcard		O	
pot		O	D
potato(es)	C	O	D
precious	C	O	D
prefer	C		D
preparation	C		D
prepare	C		D
present			D
problem	C		D
promise	C		D
pull		O	D
purple	C		
purse			D
push		O	D

	C	O	D
Q			
queen		O	D
quick			D
R			
rabbi	C		
raise			D
remember			D
remove	C		D
rent	C		D
reply(ies)			D
reporter(s)	C		
require	C		D
rest			D
restaurant	C	O	D
rice			D
rich	C		D
ride		O	D
ring		O	D
roast			D
robber			D
rock	C	O	D
rocket		O	
S			
sad			D
sand			D
sandwich		O	D
scene	C		D
science	C	O	
scientific	C		D
secret	C		D
secretary	C	O	D
section	C	O	D
selfish			D
shake(s)		O	D
sharp			D
shiny			D
shirt		O	D
shoe(maker)		O	D

Word	C	O	D
shoot			D
shop		O	D
shopping cart		O	
short		O	D
shout(s)			D
sick			D
silver			D
sink		O	D
smell(s)			D
sofa	C	O	
soft drink		O	
soldier	C	O	D
sole(s)		O	
son		O	D
sorry			D
soup	C		D
space	C	O	
speed			D
spirit	C		D
station	C	O	D
step			D
stethoscope	C	O	
stick		O	D
still			D
stomach	C	O	D
stone			D
stupid	C		D
such			D
suddenly			D
summer		O	D
supermarket	C	O	
surface			D
surprise	C		D
sympathy	C		D

T

table		O	D
tall		O	D
taste			D
tear(s) (n.)			D
teeth		O	
telephone	C	O	D
temperature	C		D

Word	C	O	D
thin		O	
though			D
throw		O	D
tie		O	D
tiny			D
tomato	C	O	
tooth		O	D
touch		O	D
towel	C	O	D
travel		O	D
trick			D
truck		O	
true			D
truth			D
twice			D

U

understand			D
unhappy			D
(un)sympathetic			D
useless			D

V

Word	C	O	D
village	C		D
volcano	C		

W

Word	C	O	D
wear			D
weather		O	D
wheelchair		O	
whisper			D
whistle		O	D
winter		O	D
wise			D
wonder			D
wonderful			D
wooden			D
worse			D

XYZ

Word	C	O	D
yet			D
young			D

Exercise Answer Key

A USELESS OLD MAN

Exercise II

1.	a		4.	c
2.	b		5.	c
3.	c		6.	b

Exercise III
1. Eva gives Bruno breakfast.
or/ She puts his binoculars near him.
or/ She makes him a sandwich.
or/ She puts the telephone near Bruno.
2. Bruno thinks he is a useless old man because he cannot walk and cannot work.
3. He speaks very little English and he is ashamed.
4. They are kissing under a tree.
5. He writes the license number on the palm of his hand.
6. Bruno tells her, "Eva, call the police."

THE MAN, THE BOY, AND THE DONKEY

Exercise II

1.	c		4.	b
2.	c		5.	c
3.	c		6.	c

Exercise III
1. The farmer and his son are going to town.
2. (He says) "A donkey is to ride on."
3. This time the farmer gets on the donkey's back.
4. (She says) "I think he's a bad father."
5. They sit down on the road and think and think for a long time.
6. He jumps off the bridge into the river and swims away.

MRS. PROCTOR GOES TO THE DOCTOR

Exercise II

1.	c		4.	c
2.	b		5.	b
3.	c		6.	b

Exercise III
1. She has to walk with a crutch.
2. Mrs. Proctor is sitting on the examination table.
3. She listens to Mrs. Proctor's heart with a stethoscope.
4. She says, "I am ninety-three years old, Doctor."
5. She is writing what Mrs. Proctor tells her as fast as she can.

COOKIES

Exercise II

1.	b		4.	b
2.	c		5.	c
3.	a		6.	b
			7.	b

Exercise III
1. He is going to talk to an important man about a job.
2. Sam is twenty years old.
3. He tells her that he is here to talk to Mr. Wilson about a job.
4. Mr. Wilson isn't back from lunch yet.
5. Sam sits in a chair.
6. She is unhappy because Mr. Wilson is late.

A PRESENT FOR PETER

Exercise II

1.	c		4.	a and b
2.	b		5.	c
3.	c		6.	a

Exercise III
1. Peter is interested in science.
2. She likes it because it is very black and very shiny.
3. The man who works in the store tells her that obsidian is glass that comes from a volcano.
4. The bus driver throws the rock over a fence into a small park.
5. He picks it up and takes it home.
6. It (the jacket) belongs to the painter.

A MOTHER AND A MOTHER-IN-LAW

Exercise II

1.	b	4.	c
2.	c	5.	b
3.	c	6.	b

Exercise III
1. She laughs to show that she is only joking.
2. Rick doesn't want his wife to work.
3. Cathy needs a lot of rest (so she sleeps until noon).
4. She goes shopping at the very best stores.
5. Patty is so lazy (that she sleeps until noon).
6. Because Patty doesn't like to cook.

STONE SOUP

Exercise II

1.	c	4.	c
2.	c	5.	a
3.	a	6.	c

Exercise III
1. They don't have horses to ride.
2. They don't know that the people in this village are selfish.
3. Leon can see roast beef and vegetables.
4. She wants to learn how to make soup from a stone.
5. He tells her, "That soup really is the best soup in the world."
6. They walk down the road laughing as hard as they can.

JACK AND THE BANDIT

Exercise II

1.	c	4.	a
2.	c	5.	c
3.	c	6.	c

Exercise III
1. (Suddenly) a bandit jumps out from behind a tree.
2. He takes his money out of his pocket and hands it to the bandit.
3. (He says), "I want to buy my wife a warm coat."
4. He wants people to think he is a dangerous man.

5.   The bandit shoots a hole in Jack's jacket.
6.   (He says) "I can't. I have no more bullets."

A BOX OF CHOCOLATES

Exercise II

1.	c		4.	c
2.	b		5.	c
3.	c		6.	b

Exercise III
1.   She is going to see her first granddaughter.
2.   The bus is more economical.
3.   She always buys picture post cards to send to her friends in Houston.
4.   She buys a small box of chocolate candy.
or/ Hershey's Kisses.
5.   He has no place to sit
6.   He throws the box away.

ROSA PARKS GOES TO JAIL

Exercise II

1.	b		4.	b
2.	a		5.	c
3.	c		6.	c

Exercise III
1.   Rosa feels (She feels) especially tired.
2.   The bus company in Montgomery makes black people sit at the back of their buses.
3.   "No, I am not."
4.   (His name is) Dr. Martin Luther King, Jr.
5.   Rosa loses her job because she works for the boycott.
6.   (The United States Constitution promises) equal rights and equal justice to everyone.

THE RABBI AND THE SHOEMAKER

Exercise II

1.	b		4.	c
2.	c		5.	c
3.	b		6.	b

Exercise III
1. The babies sleep under the trees
2. They cry day and night.
3. Everyone says this rabbi is wise and wonderful.
4. He can't hear anything.
5. She doesn't talk to Jacob.
6. It smells terrible.

MY LUCKY APARTMENT

Exercise II

1.	b	4.	a
2.	c	5.	c
3.	c	6.	c

Exercise III
1. She is wearing a blue summer dress and a white summer hat.
2. He is very interested in beautiful young women.
3. "I'm sorry. I don't have a telephone."
4. Carl has an apartment in the same building.
5. Carl shows Steve an old newspaper.
6. Gloria's white summer hat.

MAYBE SOME PARROTS NEED TO SPEAK BETTER ENGLISH

Exercise II

1.	b	4.	a
2.	b	5.	b
3.	b	6.	c

Exercise III
1. Leonard telephones his mother twice a week.
2. He sends her beautiful presents.
3. His mother (She) has enough gold bracelets.
4. She doesn't like kittens because they grow up to be cats, and cats catch birds.
5. It speaks seven languages.
6. English is the only language his mother understands.

LAUNCHING THE APOLLO 11

Exercise II

1. c
2. a
3. b

4. b
5. a
6. c

Exercise III

1. He is the commander of the spaceship Apollo 11.
2. President Kennedy decides that the United States is going to send a man to the moon and bring him back safely to earth.
3. Scientists work together to make a journey to the moon possible.
4. Apollo 11 is going to the moon at a speed of 24,000 miles an hour.
5. Collins stays in the Apollo.
   and/or
   He flies around and around the moon, waiting to take the others back to earth.
6. All three astronauts return safely to earth.

ABOUT THE AUTHOR

For many years, Judith Bailey was a teacher, and most particularly, a reading teacher, in the Los Angeles Unified School District. Under an ESAA grant, she worked with hundreds of newly arrived students who spoke little or no English. Books, reading, the whole spectrum of language arts, have been her life-long preoccupation. Before becoming a teacher, she was a story analyst and associate story editor is several motion picture studios.

She now lives in Forestville, California, where she occupies herself as a free lance writer for major educational publishers.

ABOUT THE ARTIST

Julian Smedley is an English illustrator and composer. He won a music scholarship to Radley College, and in that rural setting he developed his love for illustration. He obtained his degree in Fine Arts at the University of East Anglia. He then moved to London, where he worked as an artist in air brush, watercolor, and pen and ink media.

In 1979, he moved to the United States, to the state of Washington, and later to Berkeley, California, where he continues writing musical scores and working as a free lance graphic designer and illustrator.

Also from JAG PUBLICATIONS

JAG PUBLICATIONS E.S.L. Materials

11288 Ventura Blvd.
Studio City, CA 91604

Telephone and Fax: (818) 505-9002
info@jagpublications-esl.com